Witness to History

Civil Rights in the USA

Brendan January

09611486

www.heinemann.co.uk/library

Visit our website to find out more information about **Heinemann Library** books.

To order:

☎ Phone 44 (0) 1865 888066

🖹 Send a fax to 44 (0) 1865 314091

💻 Visit the Heinemann Bookshop at www.heinemann.co.uk/library to browse our catalogue and order online.

First published in Great Britain by Heinemann Library,
Halley Court, Jordan Hill, Oxford
OX2 8EJ, part of Harcourt Education.
Heinemann is a registered trademark of
Harcourt Education Ltd.

© Harcourt Education Ltd 2003
First published in paperback in 2004
The moral right of the proprietor has been asserted.

Produced for Heinemann by Discovery Books Ltd
Editorial: Sarah Eason and Gill Humphrey
Design: Ian Winton
Picture Research: Rachel Tisdale
Production: Edward Moore

Originated by Ambassador Litho Ltd
Printed and bound in Hong Kong, China
by South China Printing

ISBN 0 431 17044 4 (hardback)
07 06 05 04 03
10 9 8 7 6 5 4 3 2 1

ISBN 0 431 17050 9 (paperback)
08 07 06 05 04
10 9 8 7 6 5 4 3 2 1

British Library Cataloguing in Publication Data
January, Brendan
  Civil Rights in the USA. – (Witness to History)
  323'.0973
A full catalogue record for this book is available from the British Library.

Acknowledgements
The publishers would like to thank the following for permission to reproduce photographs:
Bettmann/Corbis pp.4, 5, 13, 19, 21, 23, 24, 25, 26, 28, 29, 31, 32, 34, 36, 40, 41, 42, 43, 43, 44; Corbis pp.10, 15, 16, 38; Corbis/Flip Schulk p.30; Corbis/Ariel Skelley p.48; Corbis Sygma/Rubin Steven p.50; Peter Newark's Historical Pictures pp.6, 8, 9, 11, 14, 33, 45; Popperfoto/Reuters p.46.

Cover photograph shows civil rights protesters taking part in the March on Washington in 1963, reproduced with permission of Corbis.

The publishers would like to thank Bob Rees, historian and assistant head teacher, for his assistance in the preparation of this book.

Disclaimer
All Internet addresses (URLs) given in this book were valid at the time of going to press. However, due to the dynamic nature of the Internet, some addresses may have changed, or sites may have changed or ceased to exist since publication. While the author and publisher regret any inconvenience this may cause readers, no responsibility for any such changes can be accepted by either the author or the publisher.

Every effort has been made to contact copyright holders of any material reproduced in this book. Any omissions will be rectified in subsequent printings if notice is given to the publishers.

Words appearing in bold, **like this,** are explained in the Glossary.

Contents

Introduction 4
How do we know? 6
Slavery 8
Resistance and rebellion 10
Civil war and Reconstruction 12
Jim Crow 14
Calls for equal rights 16
Brown vs. Board of Education of Topeka 18
Rosa Parks 20
The Montgomery bus boycott 22
Showdown at Little Rock 24
Non-violent resistance 26
Freedom Rides 28
The battle of Birmingham 30
The children's march 32
March on Washington 34
Freedom Summer 36
Civil Rights Act 38
Slow to change 40
Malcolm X and black power 42
Assassinations and riots 44
Civil rights in the 1970s, 1980s and 1990s 46
The unfinished revolution 48
What have we learnt from the
    Civil Rights Movement? 50
Timeline 52
Find out more 53
List of primary sources 54
Glossary 55
Index 56

Introduction

In the 1950s, black Americans and their supporters began an epic struggle to win **equality** in the United States. They demanded the freedoms most white Americans took for granted, like the right to vote and the right to the protection of the law. Black Americans wanted the same opportunities as whites, an equal chance of getting good jobs, nice homes and good schools for their children. They fought to be treated as equal to the white majority.

Through marches and **rallies**, in the courts and on the streets, black Americans broke down a system of laws and attitudes that had largely confined them to a lower position in American society. Today, that struggle is called the 'Civil Rights Movement'.

A non-violent protest

The Civil Rights Movement was marked by extraordinary bravery and guided mostly by the idea of **non-violence** and **civil disobedience**. Demonstrators marched in small groups or in the hundreds of thousands. They clapped, chanted and sang songs that cried out for freedom. They disobeyed laws that were unfair or took away their rights. One of the movement's most important leaders, Martin Luther King Jr., urged his followers not to fight back if they were hit, cursed at, or attacked. Violence, he said, would only lead to more pain and bloodshed.

Even in the 1950s some black Americans still struggled in a state of near slavery with little access to schooling, medical care or the protection of the law. In 1958 this family of **migrant workers** lived in a small one-roomed wooden shack in Virginia while they worked temporarily on a farm. After the harvest, they would have to move on to find more work.

In 1965, Martin Luther King led an 86-kilometre (54-mile) march from Selma to Montgomery, Alabama, where he demanded that Governor George Wallace stop police brutality and help black Americans exercise their right to vote.

King's words were deeply important because the Civil Rights Movement was bitterly resisted. For hundreds of years white Americans had enjoyed more rights than black Americans. Sadly, many white Americans still believed they were superior to blacks and didn't want change. On one occasion firefighters were ordered to turn their powerful hoses on crowds of black marchers and police unleashed snarling attack dogs, but the protests could not be stopped.

Changing attitudes

The civil rights demonstrators carried on their protests even when they faced angry white mobs. Demonstrations still continued after many civil rights leaders were murdered, and Martin Luther King, the leading voice in the Civil Rights Movement, was **assassinated**. In the end the Movement led to new laws being introduced that protected black Americans' rights. Even more important, many people embraced new attitudes about what it meant to be white, black and American. By the end of the 1960s, the United States had been changed for ever.

How do we know?

Historians examine **primary sources** – documents, recordings, or objects – to reconstruct and tell of the past. Newspapers are excellent primary sources. They provide dramatic accounts of events as they occurred. Letters and diaries reveal how people felt and thought as history unfolded around them. Speeches are more formal and provide a record of how leaders publicly sought or created change. Photographs provide memorable images of figures and scenes. In more recent times film footage has captured historical events as they happened, as when President John F. Kennedy was **assassinated** in 1963, or when the World Trade Center was attacked by terrorists in September 2001.

The power of primary sources

The Civil Rights Movement developed at a time when television was becoming popular and more common. For the first time, millions of people could see moving images of an event almost as it occurred. What they saw would determine how the nation's leaders reacted to events, especially the Civil Rights Movement. These images are also valuable historical **artefacts** that are carefully studied today.

Historians also seek out stories and accounts given by people who were involved in movements and events at that time. These accounts, called oral history, give a very personal and intimate view of the Civil Rights Movement.

Getting to the truth

Primary sources can be biased or inaccurate. Some sources are created quickly, just after a violent event. People forget or confuse facts and they misspell names. They may make mistakes or just not remember properly. Sometimes people have prejudices or opinions that may influence the way they report an event. If someone dislikes the government, for example, then they are less likely to give an **unbiased** account of that government's activities. It is the historian's job to carefully read through the sources and determine what is most accurate. They can compare sources to judge what actually occurred. To research the Civil Rights Movement, historians also look to **secondary sources**. These are sources that come to the historian second-hand. They are often accounts written long after the events took place. Historians, today and in the future, will use primary and secondary sources to tell the story of the Civil Rights Movement. This is how they write the history that appears in books, textbooks and magazines. They will use the sources to write descriptions, narrate events and answer important questions, such as what was the US like before the Movement, what happened during it, and what have we become since?

Televisions became a common item in American households during the 1950s and 1960s. Through television the entire nation was able to see first-hand the images of interracial violence, warfare and speeches from national leaders, such as John F. Kennedy in this picture.

Slavery

Unlike almost every other group of people that came to North America, black Americans were taken from Africa against their will. The first Africans were unloaded in chains in Jamestown, Virginia, in 1619, just a decade after a group of English people founded the settlement. The colony desperately needed people to clear thick forests and plant crops such as tobacco.

Slavery has existed throughout history. In many cultures, slaves were allowed to earn their freedom or could keep their children from being enslaved. In the Americas, however, slavery evolved into a particularly brutal form. Slavery was identified by black skin colour and children of slaves were kept in **bondage**.

By the early 1800s, slavery had spread throughout the United States. Slaves were loaded on to boats, mainly on the West African coast (in present-day countries such as Angola, Nigeria, Ivory Coast and Sierra Leone), and taken across the Atlantic Ocean to southern US ports. There, the slaves were unloaded and sold in large markets. Slaves performed all kinds of tasks, from toiling in cotton fields to cooking in **plantation** mansions. They had no rights and it was illegal for whites to teach blacks to read or write. Slaves were treated as property, like a wagon or a horse. Punishment for disobedience could be severe, from a light whipping to death.

A slave market in Virginia during the 1850s. Having been taken by force from their home country, this African family then had to face the humiliation of being sold at a slave market.

Olaudah Equiano's account

Olaudah Equiano was born in 1745 in what is now Nigeria. He was forced into slavery at just eleven years old. Eventually he bought his freedom and moved to England. Equiano was one of the few slaves able to write about his life as a slave. In 1789 he published *The Interesting Narrative of the Life of Olaudah Equiano, or Gustavus Vassa, Written by Himself*. In this extract he describes his experience of boarding a slave ship.

The first object which saluted my eyes when I arrived on the coast was the sea, and a slave ship, which was then riding at anchor, and waiting for its cargo. These filled me with astonishment, which was soon converted into terror. When I was carried on board, I was immediately handled, and tossed up, to see if I were sound [healthy], by some of the crew; and I was now persuaded that I had gotten into a world of bad spirits and that they were going to kill me. Their complexions too differing so much from ours, their long hair and the language they spoke which was very different from any I had ever heard united me to this belief.

Olaudah Equiano is painted here wearing the clothes of an English gentleman.

Resistance and rebellion

By the mid 1800s, around 4 million slaves lived in the United States, mostly in the South. In the houses of the cities and among the rows of slave shacks on **plantations**, slaves resisted their **bondage**.

Many slaves decided to seize freedom by escaping to the northern states, where slavery was outlawed (by 1860). Some free blacks and northern whites helped slaves escape north by establishing an 'underground railroad'. The railroad was actually a series of safe hiding places, where escaping slaves could spend the night before resuming their journey north.

Freed slaves faced severe **discrimination** in the northern states as well, but they could move about freely. As a result some free blacks got together and began publishing newspapers and holding **rallies** demanding the **abolition** of slavery.

Other resistance to slavery was more violent. On 21 August 1831, in Southampton County in the state of Virginia, a slave named Nat Turner and a group of other slaves seized weapons and began attacking white households. By the time Turner and his 75 followers were killed or captured, 60 whites had been killed. The **rebellion** shook the white South to its core. Before Nat Turner, many white southerners had believed slaves were simple people who were content, even happy, with their situation. Turner showed this attitude to be a myth.

Henry Bibb's letter
The slave, Henry Bibb, escaped to Detroit, and he wrote this letter in 1844 to his former master.

Frederick Douglass, an escaped slave, wrote a masterful narrative about his experiences and led the fight against slavery through his newspaper, the *North Star*. The paper was named after the star escaped slaves used to direct themselves northwards to freedom.

Many slaves tried to escape their miserable situation. Plantation owners regularly placed advertisements in the newspaper that described the features and character of the slave, along with a reward for his or her return.

I thank God that I am not property now, but am regarded as a man like yourself, and although I live far north, I am enjoying a comfortable living by my own industry. If you should ever chance to be travelling this way, and will call on me, I will use you better than you did me while you held me as a slave. Think not that I have any malice against you, for the cruel treatment which you inflicted on me while I was in your power. As it was the custom of your country, to treat your fellow men as you did me and my little family, I can freely forgive you.

You may perhaps think hard of us for running away from slavery, but as to myself, I have but one apology to make for it, which is this: I have only to regret that I did not start at an earlier period. I might have been free long before I was.

Civil war and Reconstruction

The issue of slavery bitterly divided the northern and the southern states. Free blacks in the North, and many whites as well, saw it as a brutal and savage system. Southern whites angrily defended it as their way of life. Equally important was the fact that the entire economy of the South depended on slavery. It was slaves that worked the **plantations**, the mines and any manufacturing industries. When Abraham Lincoln was elected president in 1860, he promised to **abolish** slavery. The southern states decided to **secede** and the nation disintegrated into bloody **civil war**.

Around 180,000 blacks served in the **Union** army and navy during the American Civil War, which lasted from 1861 to 1865. In January 1863 the Emancipation Proclamation, was issued, which eventually brought about the downfall of slavery. As the northern Union armies advanced into the South, thousands of slaves fled the plantations. When the war ended with northern victory, former slaves, now called 'freedmen', joyfully embraced freedom.

Letters from slaves
These letters written after the abolition of slavery give us a clear picture of the how slaves felt at being free.

The defeated southern states were brought back into the Union in a process called **Reconstruction**. To re-enter the Union, white southerners had to give their former slaves new rights. Three amendments (changes or additions) were added to the **Constitution** – the 13th, 14th and 15th – that abolished slavery and gave the freedmen the right to vote and the protection of the law.

To the fury of the southern whites, Union soldiers carrying rifles and bayonets were stationed throughout the South to guarantee the freedmen's rights. In 1877, as part of a deal to elect the northern Rutherford B. Hayes as president, the Union soldiers were pulled out of the southern states. Southern whites regained control, and they had no intention of treating their former slaves as equals.

Former slave, Robert Purvis, wrote about the changes in the country during the civil war.

This photograph, taken during the American Civil War, shows escaped slaves on a plantation that had been captured by Union soldiers. The escaped slaves are sorting through clumps of picked cotton.

Dear Mrs Cheney,

I felt I would like to write to you a line from my old home. I am sitting under the old roof twelve feet from the spot where I suffered all the crushing weight of slavery. Thank God the bitter cup is drained of its last dreg. There is no need for more hiding places.

I cannot tell you how I feel in this place. The change is so great I can hardly take it all in. I was born here . . . I have hunted up all the old people, done what I could for them . . . many of them I have known since childhood.

I never saw such a state of excitement . . .

_____

Hi Jacobs

Sir, old things are passing away, all things are becoming new. Now a black man has rights, under this government, which every white man, here and everywhere, is bound to respect . . . The slave power no longer rules in Washington. The slaveholders and their miserable allies are biting the dust.

Jim Crow

With the **Union** troops gone, white southerners moved quickly to return blacks to a state of near slavery. They created laws called 'Jim Crow' that took away the rights black Americans had recently been guaranteed in the **Constitution**. These laws kept black Americans from owning property, taking good paying jobs or testifying in court against a white person. From the late 1880s to the early 1900s the South turned itself into a society where blacks and whites were kept apart by a system of **segregation**.

No part of southern life was left untouched by Jim Crow. All public places in the South were divided by race: public lavatories, trains, courts, theatres, schools, buses, sports leagues, even parks and swimming areas. Southern whites insisted that segregation was fair. They said the races were 'separate but equal'. In reality, however, this was rarely true. For example, even though both blacks and whites paid taxes, white schools were better built and received more tax money.

Those who challenged Jim Crow were often denied jobs and loans from the local banks. Others were arrested, beaten or killed. White groups, such as the **Ku Klux Klan**, used murder and violence to bully blacks into submission. Black Americans battled against Jim Crow from the start. They insisted that separating the races broke the law. But in 1896, the **Supreme Court** issued a crushing decision called *Plessy vs. Ferguson* that supported Jim Crow.

The Ku Klux Klan, shown here marching through a southern town in 1925, have been guilty of using violence and murder in support of their belief that white people were superior to black people, and that the races should be strictly segregated.

John Marshall Harlan angrily disagrees with Supreme Court ruling

Supreme Court Justice John Marshall Harlan, disagreed with the *Plessy vs. Ferguson* ruling of 1896 that said separating the races was legal as long as conditions were equal.

The white race deems itself to be the dominant race in this country. But in the view of the Constitution, in the eye of the law, there is in this country no superior, dominant ruling class of citizens. Our Constitution is color-blind. In respect of civil rights, all citizens are equal before the law. It is, therefore, to be regretted that [the Supreme Court] has reached the conclusion to regulate civil rights solely upon the basis of race.

We boast of the freedom enjoyed by our people above all other peoples. But it is difficult to reconcile that boast with a law which, practically, puts the brand of servitude [near slavery] and degradation [humiliation] upon a large class of our fellow-citizens. The thin disguise of 'equal' accommodations will not mislead anyone, nor atone for the wrong this day done.

Supreme Court Justice John Marshall Harlan was disgusted when the Supreme Court upheld segregation in an 1896 decision. He believed that all US citizens should be 'equal before the law'.

15

Calls for equal rights

Racism and **segregation** were not just limited to the South. Blacks faced **discrimination** across the country. Schools were segregated throughout the South and in many states in the North and West, including New Jersey and California. Blacks were routinely shut out of good paying jobs and leadership positions.

Through the late 1800s and into the 1900s, hundreds of black individuals and organizations battled racism and discrimination. Many black leaders, like Mary McLeod Bethune and Booker T. Washington, believed that education would overcome racism. W. E. B. Du Bois, a writer and **activist**, helped found the National Association for the Advancement of Colored People (NAACP) in 1909 to 'promote **equality** of rights and eradicate [remove] race prejudice among the citizens of the United States'. Supported by both black and white activists, the organization battled against laws that kept black Americans out of good housing, schools and jobs.

Black Americans who had served in segregated units in World War I (1914–18) returned home to find that little had changed. They still had to eat in separate sections and drink from separate water fountains.

The National Association for the Advancement of Colored People was one of the most important organizations to battle racism in the United States. In this photo from the 1930s, a Youth Council from the Association urges others to join their cause.

Reverend Ralph Abernathy describes segregation in the South

Ralph Abernathy, who later worked with Martin Luther King, gives an account of what life was like for blacks living in the segregated southern states.

Blacks were permitted to hold only the menial jobs, domestic workers and common and ordinary labourers. The only professional jobs that were open to blacks were ... pastoring a black church and the school teaching profession, which was open because of segregated schools. White teachers didn't normally teach black students. In the whole state of Alabama we had probably less than five black doctors. And we didn't do anything but dig ditches and work with some white supervisor that told us everything to do. We were the last to be hired and the first to be fired.

All of the restaurants were segregated, the hotels and motels were segregated. Meaning that black people were not permitted to live in these hotels. Even in the public courthouse, blacks could not drink water except from the fountain labeled 'Colored.' You could not use a filling station that was not designated with a restroom [toilets] for colored. You had a restroom for white males and a restroom for white women, and you had a restroom for colored. Meaning that colored people had to use the same restroom, male and female. And the janitor [cleaner] never would clean up the restroom for the colored people.

Brown vs. Board of Education of Topeka

The NAACP decided to use the law to fight **segregation**. In the 1930s, NAACP lawyers brought cases to court to show that segregated schools were unequal and crippled the education of black American students. Black students also took matters into their own hands. In April 1951, 450 black students at a Moton High School in Farmville, Virginia, walked out of their school. They protested that their school had no cafeteria, no gym and was crowded with twice as many students as the building could safely hold. Moton High School teachers were paid far less than the white teachers who taught at the local white high school.

The issues raised by the Moton High School students applied to hundreds of other US schools. The NAACP, through a group called the Legal Defense Fund, filed more and more lawsuits. One case was brought against the Board of Education in Topeka, Kansas. Oliver Brown, a black resident, was angered that his seven-year-old daughter had to travel across town to a black school. Another school was much closer, but it was for white students only.

By 1952, Brown's case and several others were being heard by the **Supreme Court**. Standing before the court in Washington, D.C., the NAACP lawyers argued that separating black students made them feel inferior. 'Separate but equal', they argued, wasn't possible. On 17 May 1954, the Supreme Court announced a decision in the *Brown vs. Board of Education of Topeka* case. Stunning the nation, the justices wrote that segregation did **discriminate** against black students. Segregation in schools, the court ruled, was against the law. The victory launched the Civil Rights Movement.

Earl Warren announces Supreme Court's decision

Earl Warren, a Supreme Court Judge, read out the ruling on the *Brown vs. Board of Topeka* case which overturned the idea of 'separate but equal' in education.

This is a segregated school in Uno, Virginia, in 1947. Black students went to separate schools and were taught by black teachers. White students attended their own schools, which were always better funded and had better facilities.

Does segregation of children in public schools solely on the basis of race deprive children of the minority group of equal educational opportunities? We believe it does. To separate them from others of similar age and qualifications solely because of their race generates a feeling of inferiority as to their status in the community that may affect their hearts and minds in a way very unlikely to be undone. We conclude unanimously, that in the field of public education the doctrine of 'separate but equal' has no place. Separate educational facilities are inherently unequal.

Rosa Parks

The **Supreme Court's** decision was just a beginning. **Segregation** in schools was declared illegal, but segregation still existed almost everywhere else, from theatres to swimming pools.

On buses throughout the South, white people sat in the front; black people at the back. Bus segregation was especially humiliating to black Americans. If the black section filled up, black riders couldn't sit in the white section, even if seats were available. If the bus was crowded, blacks were forced to give their seats to whites. On 1 December 1955, a 43-year-old black woman named Rosa Parks boarded a bus in Montgomery, Alabama. Exhausted after a long day, Parks sat down. The bus continued on its route and filled up with passengers. When a white man boarded, the bus driver turned around and ordered Parks to give up her seat. Parks refused and was arrested. Her simple act of defiance inspired an entire city and later an entire country.

Montgomery's black community was outraged that Parks, a hardworking quiet woman, had been arrested. Many black groups and ministers who had looked to challenge bus segregation now decided to take a stand. They selected a leader, a 26-year-old minister named Martin Luther King Jr.

This maps shows the states that formed the Confederacy during the Civil War and which are today referred to as the 'South'.

Key

Present-day states which made up the Confederate States of America or 'South' during the American Civil War (1861–65)

Boston

Chicago

New York City

UNITED STATES OF AMERICA

Washington DC

VIRGINIA

Greensboro

Raleigh

TENNESSEE   N. CAROLINA

ARKANSAS   Memphis   S. CAROLINA

Birmingham   Atlanta

Little Rock

MISSISSIPPI   Selma   Montgomery

TEXAS   Jackson   ALABAMA   Albany

LOUISIANA   GEORGIA

St Augustine

New Orleans

FLORIDA

N

0   800 km   W   E

0   500 miles   S

Exhausted after a long day, Rosa Parks was arrested after refusing to give up her bus seat to a white man. In this photograph she stands with her **attorney** after being released from jail.

Rosa Parks's account

In an interview given some years after the event, Rosa Parks recalls the moment when she refused to give up her bus seat.

This one man was standing and when the driver looked around and saw he was standing he asked the four of us, the man in the seat with me and the two women across the aisle, to let him have those front seats. At his first request, didn't any of us move. Then he spoke again and said 'You'd better make it light on yourselves and let me have those seats' . . . When the three people stood up and moved into the aisle, I remained where I was. When the driver saw that I was still sitting there, he asked if I was going to stand up. I told him, no, I wasn't. He said, 'Well, if you don't stand up, I'm going to have you arrested.' I told him to go on and have me arrested.

The Montgomery bus boycott

King and other black Montgomery leaders decided to launch a **boycott** of the city's buses. The boycott was organized by the Montgomery Improvement Association (MIA). By refusing to ride the buses, the boycotters hoped the bus companies would lose money and be forced to abandon their **segregation** policy.

Montgomery's white leaders laughed at the idea of the boycott, predicting that it would quickly fail. After all, many of Montgomery's black residents relied on the buses to shop, visit friends and get to and from work.

But on 5 December 1955, the first day of the boycott, the buses pulled up to normally packed stops. This time there were few riders. The buses continued on, their seats empty. Black taxi drivers and residents with cars began a car-pool system to carry riders where they needed to go. Others simply walked. Montgomery's white leaders were enraged and baffled, but refused to give in. In February 1956, angry whites bombed several black leaders' homes. King was arrested and jailed.

But the tactics failed. Inspired by King's leadership and speeches, the Montgomery black community held firm. In November 1956, the **Supreme Court** ruled that segregation on buses was illegal. After more than a year, black residents boarded the buses again, free to sit wherever they wished. After the success of the boycott an organization called the Southern Christian Leadership Conference (SCLC) was formed to coordinate more protests. Martin Luther King was elected as its first president.

Virginia Durr describes her feelings

Not all whites were against the boycott. Virginia Durr, who lived in Montgomery at that time, believed that a great injustice had been removed.

Martin Luther King, shown here seated on the left and wearing a hat, was chosen leader of the Montgomery Improvement Association, the organization that protested against segregation on city buses. King's leadership and the success of the boycott would catapault him on to the national stage and make him one of the greatest leaders of the civil rights era.

Jo Ann Robinson describes her feelings
After the success of the boycott, many black Americans felt that they had a new power to force change in America. **Activist** Jo Ann Robinson described this feeling of power and joy.

We felt that we were somebody. That somebody has listened to us, that we had forced the white man to give what we knew was our own citizenship. And if you have never had the feeling that you are no longer an alien, but that this is your country too, then you don't know what I am talking about. It is a hilarious feeling that just goes all over you, that makes you feel that America is a great country and we're going to do more to make it greater.

When I heard that the boycott had been successful, I felt pure, unadulterated joy. It was like a fountain of joy. Of course the blacks felt that way, but the white friends I had felt the way I did. We felt joy and release. It was as if a great burden had fallen off us.

Showdown at Little Rock

Despite the *Brown vs. Board of Education* decision, **segregated** schools remained all over the USA. In Little Rock, capital of Arkansas, white mothers fiercely protested the proposed **desegregation** of the High School. Arkansas governor Orval Faubus stepped in.

As term began, Faubus called in the National Guard, to surround the school, and barred its new black students, claiming it was for their own safety. The next morning, 4 September 1957, nine black students showed up at the school. A furious mob threatened them, and the soldiers turned the students away. Two weeks later, the **NAACP** succeeded in a legal action to stop Faubus from using the National Guard this way. On 23 September, the students were taken into the school by a side door. The rage outside was so great that by mid-morning they had to leave. Infuriated, US president Dwight Eisenhower sent **federal** troops to act as personal guards for the 'Little Rock Nine', and on 24 September they started their school term, taken to and from class by armed soldiers.

One of the 'Little Rock Nine', Elizabeth Eckford, tries to ignore the taunts that come from a crowd of whites as she walks to the entrance of Little Rock High School on 4 September 1957. She would not be allowed to enter school on that day.

These federal troops ordered to Little Rock by President Eisenhower, surround Little Rock High School to make sure that black students could safely attend class. The soldiers picked up each student at the beginning of the school day, took them to their classes and drove them home in the afternoon.

Elizabeth Eckford's account

Elizabeth Eckford, one of the original nine Little Rock students, spoke about the first terrifying moments when she arrived alone at the school.

All I could hear was the shuffling of their feet. Then someone shouted, Here she comes, get ready! The crowd moved in closer and then began to follow me, calling me names. I still wasn t afraid. Just a little bit nervous. Then my knees started to shake all of a sudden and I wondered whether I could make the center entrance a block away. It was the longest block I ever walked in my whole life. I walked until I was right in front of the path to the front door. I stood looking at the school — it looked so big! Just then the guards let some white students through. The crowd was quiet. I guess they were waiting to see what was going to happen. When I was able to steady my knees, I walked up to the guard who had let the white students in. He too didn t move. When I tried to squeeze past him, he raised his bayonet and then the other guards moved in and they raised their bayonets. They glared at me with a mean look and I was very frightened and didn t know what to do.

Non-violent resistance

Protests against **segregation** broke out in cities across the United States. Most of these first protests were **non-violent**. By remaining non-violent, the demonstrators hoped to show the justice of their cause and change the minds of those who resisted change. Many civil rights leaders had been influenced by Mohandas Gandhi, whose peaceful demonstrations had helped bring about India's independence from British rule in 1947.

An example of non-violent resistance were 'sit-ins'. Restaurants in many parts of the country, including New York City, still seated blacks and whites in separate sections. Groups of black students broke down segregation by sitting in the white section and ordering food. When they were refused, as usually happened, they would not leave. They simply sat there, expressing their protest by sitting. The first sit-in occurred in Greensboro, North Carolina, in 1960.

Though sit-ins were non-violent, the reaction was often not. Students were cursed at, pelted with food, and sometimes beaten. Often they were arrested and jailed by police for disturbing the peace. The sit-in participants were taught not to respond to taunts. They were told to shield themselves and stay in their seats.

The sit-ins spread to cities around the country, with thousands of students participating. In 1960, the students who participated in the sit-ins formed their own organization – the Student Non-violent Coordinating Committee (SNCC).

Sit-in protesters at a lunch counter in Jackson, Mississippi in May 1963. One of the protesters has been covered in sugar and ketchup thrown by people in the crowd.

Franklin McCain's experience

Franklin McCain, who took part in a sit-in, describes the moments right after he and a friend sat in the 'white' section of a restaurant and ordered food.

We went over to the counter and asked to be served coffee and doughnuts. As anticipated, the reply was, 'I'm sorry we don't serve you here.' The attendant or waitress was a little bit dumbfounded. At that point there was a policeman who had walked in off the street, who was pacing the aisle behind us, where we were seated, with his club in his hand, just sort of knocking it in his hand, and just looking mean and red and little bit upset and little bit disgusted. And you had the feeling that for the first time this big bad man with the gun and the club has been pushed in a corner and he's got absolutely no defense, and the thing that's killing him more than anything else – he doesn't know what he can or what he cannot do. He's defenseless. Usually his defense is offense, and we've provoked him, yes, but we haven't provoked him outwardly enough for him to resort to violence. And I think this is just killing him; you can see it all over him.

Freedom Rides

The battle against **segregation** was taken to the nation's interstate bus system. The **Supreme Court** had ruled that segregation on buses that travelled across state lines was against the law. But segregation still existed. When buses crossed from northern states into southern states, black and white people had to move to separate sections. When the buses stopped at stations in the South, passengers still faced segregated toilets, waiting areas and drinking fountains.

In spring 1961, a group of people from the Congress of Racial **Equality** (CORE) decided to **desegregate** the nation's long-distance bus service. On 4 May 1961, thirteen white and black CORE members boarded a bus in Washington D.C. They called themselves 'Freedom Riders' and they refused to sit according to race.

The Freedom Riders were not welcome. In Anniston, Alabama, an angry crowd pelted the bus with stones and slashed the tyres. When the bus raced out of the town and stopped for the tyres to be changed, the mob followed and threw a fire bomb into the front door. The riders escaped as the bus burned. Despite the violence, the Freedom Rides continued. More riders followed, many were attacked and beaten. Others were jailed. But after the long summer of 1961, segregation on the nation's interstate buses could not survive. It came to an end in September 1961 after a ruling from the Interstate Commerce Commission.

This photograph captures the moments after a white mob caught up with a bus carrying 'Freedom Riders' into the South. The bus boils with smoke and flames started by angry whites. Freedom Riders sit in the foreground.

On 20 May 1961, Jim Zwerg, a white Freedom Rider, was beaten in Montgomery, Alabama by a group of whites. Lying in a hospital bed and covered with cuts and bruises, he spoke to a reporter.

Segregation must be stopped. It must be broken down. Those of us who are on the Freedom Rides will continue. I'm not sure if I'll be able to, but we are going on to New Orleans no matter what happens. We are dedicated to this. We will take hitting. We'll take beatings. We're willing to accept death. But we are going to keep coming until we can ride from anywhere in the South to anyplace else in the South, as Americans, without anyone making any comment.

Jim Zwerg, a 21-year-old Freedom Rider, lies in a hospital bed after being beaten by a mob of whites at a Montgomery bus terminal. Despite his injuries, Zwerg vowed that segregation would have to stop.

The battle of Birmingham

Martin Luther King called Birmingham, Alabama, 'probably the most thoroughly **segregated** city in the United States'. In 1963, virtually every facility, from buses to theatres to drinking fountains, separated the 350,000 black and white residents. Declaring that 'as Birmingham goes, so goes the South', King was determined to shatter segregation in the city.

In spring 1963, King began organizing protests and **picketing** of city businesses. The Southern Christian Leadership Conference (SCLC) produced a list of demands which, if followed, would bring about **desegregation**. King was arrested and sent to jail. In a newspaper article, a group of Birmingham business, religious and civic leaders, called King a troublemaker and urged him to stop demonstrating against segregation. Instead, they said, King should be more patient and wait for change.

King, alone in his jail cell, wrote a letter in response to this attack. The document, 'Letter from a Birmingham Jail', has become a classic in the writings of the Civil Rights Movement.

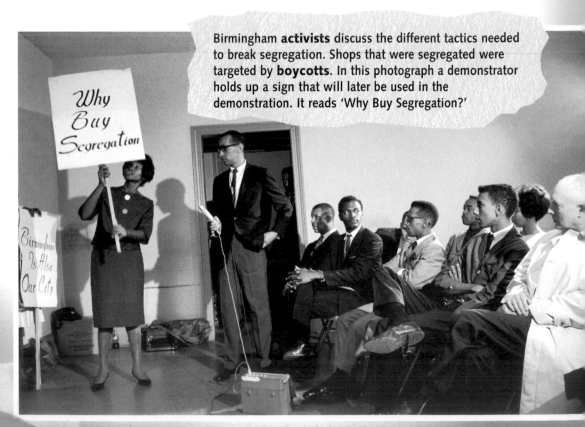

Birmingham **activists** discuss the different tactics needed to break segregation. Shops that were segregated were targeted by **boycotts**. In this photograph a demonstrator holds up a sign that will later be used in the demonstration. It reads 'Why Buy Segregation?'

Martin Luther King writes from jail

Here is an excerpt from King's letter explaining why black Americans were no longer content to wait.

For years now I have heard the word 'Wait!' It rings in the ear of every Negro [African American] with piercing familiarity. This 'Wait' has always meant 'Never.' We have waited more than 340 years for our constitutional and God-given rights. Perhaps it is easy for those who have never felt the stinging darts of segregation to say, 'Wait.' But . . . when you suddenly find your tongue twisted and your speech stammering as you seek to explain to your six-year-old daughter why she can't go to the public amusement park that has just been advertised on television, and see tears welling up in her eyes when she is told that Funtown is closed to colored children, and see ominous clouds of inferiority beginning to form in her little mental sky, and see her beginning to distort her personality by developing an unconscious bitterness toward white people; when you take a cross-country drive and find it necessary to sleep night after night in the uncomfortable corners of your automobile because no motel will accept you; when you are humiliated day in and day out by nagging signs reading 'white' and 'colored'; when you are fighting a degenerating [gradually worsening] sense of 'nobodiness'- then you will understand why we find it so difficult to wait.

Martin Luther King was often arrested and taken to jail. King used his own imprisonment to draw attention to his cause. He also wrote eloquent defences of his tactics, such as the classic 'Letter from a Birmingham Jail'.

The children's march

With King in jail, the protests in Birmingham began to collapse. Sensing a crisis, civil rights leaders in Birmingham decided on a new strategy. A group of black children would march in Birmingham to protest against **racism**. If the children of Birmingham couldn't awaken America's conscience, they thought, then nothing would.

On 2 May 1963, the children, aged six and over, marched, singing and clapping. Almost 1000 were arrested and taken to jail. The next day, the city's commissioner of public safety, Bull Connor, ordered the city's firemen to direct powerful hoses at the children. The jets of water blasted them against buildings and knocked them down. Shocked and enraged, Birmingham's black community turned out in their thousands the next day. This time the demonstrators were met by growling attack dogs as well as fire hoses.

The photographs of demonstrators huddling along walls and by trees were seen in newspapers and on televisions around the world. Feelings of disgust and rage from around the nation descended on Birmingham. President John F. Kennedy had sympathized with the black cause, but had not wanted to upset southern white voters. After Birmingham, however, he quickly realized something had to be done.

Three civil rights demonstrators cling to each other as they are blasted with water from fire hoses. Images like this one, taken during the protests in Birmingham in May 1963, were shown on television screens and in newspapers around the world.

President John F. Kennedy's speech

A few weeks after the children's march, on 11 June 1963, President Kennedy delivered a national speech that promised to introduce new **legislation** in support of civil rights.

The heart of the question is whether all Americans are to be afforded equal rights and equal opportunities; whether we are going to treat our fellow Americans as we want to be treated.

If an American, because his skin is dark, cannot eat lunch in a restaurant open to the public; if he cannot send his children to the best public schools available; if he cannot vote for the public officials who represent him; if, in short, he cannot enjoy the full and free life which all of us want, then who among us would be content to have the color of his skin changed and stand in his place?

Who among us would then be content with the counsels of patience and delay? One hundred years of delay have passed since President Lincoln freed the slaves, yet their heirs, their grandsons, are not fully free...

And this nation, for all its hopes and all its boasts, will not be fully free until all its citizens are free. Now the time has come for the nation to fulfill its promise.

President John F. Kennedy, like Eisenhower before him, was at first reluctant to involve the national government in the civil rights controversy. But the violence that surrounded the demonstrations in Birmingham forced him to call for new civil rights legislation.

March on Washington

With the confrontation in Birmingham still smouldering, Kennedy introduced **legislation** into **Congress** to abolish **segregation** in public places and **discrimination** in the job market. As the legislation was being debated in the halls of Congress, black leaders decided to organize a mass demonstration in the nation's capital. The 'March on Washington' would show the nation and its leaders the vital importance of civil rights. The leaders called for the march to take place at the end of August 1963.

News of the march spread and thousands of blacks and white supporters planned to attend. Dozens of trains and more than 2000 buses were used to transport marchers from different parts of the country. On 28 August more than 250,000 demonstrators filled the National Mall in front of the Lincoln Memorial.

Dozens of speakers gave speeches at a podium set before the statue of Abraham Lincoln. Many remarked that it had been 100 years since the Emancipation Proclamation was signed, which eventually ended slavery in the South.

At the end of the day, Martin Luther King gave the 'I Have a Dream' speech. In it, he described his hope that the USA would become a nation that honoured the rights of all its citizens, regardless of their skin colour.

August 1963: Martin Luther King stands before a crowd of hundreds of thousands on Washington D.C.'s National Mall and delivers the 'I Have a Dream' speech. The speech, in which King called for a colour-blind society built on trust and love, has become a classic statement of the Civil Rights Movement.

So I say to you, my friends, that even though we must face the difficulties of today and tomorrow, I still have a dream. It is a dream deeply rooted in the American dream that one day this nation will rise up and live out the true meaning of its creed — 'We hold these truths to be self evident that all men are created equal.'

I have a dream that one day on the red hills of Georgia, sons of former slaves and sons of former slave owners will be able to sit down together at the table of brotherhood.

I have a dream that one day, even the state of Mississippi, a state sweltering with the heat of oppression, will be transformed into an oasis of freedom and justice.

I have a dream that my four little children will one day live in a nation where they will not be judged by the color of their skin, but by the content of their character. I have a dream today!

Freedom Summer

In 1964, **activists** launched a bold campaign to end **segregation** in Mississippi, a state in the heartland of the South. Civil rights leaders invited black and white students from around the country to come to Mississippi. In a project called 'Freedom Summer', hundreds of students, mostly from the north-east, answered the call. The students spread out into the Mississippi countryside, trying to register blacks to vote. In the 1950s only five per cent of voting age blacks were registered to vote. Many more wanted to register, but worried that if they did they might lose their jobs. With the power to vote, the civil rights activists hoped that black Mississippians could influence political decision-making in their state.

White Mississippians regarded the Freedom Summer project as a hostile invasion by outsiders. The mayor of Jackson city, Allen Thompson, expanded the police force, purchased 250 shotguns and planned to use the nearby fairgrounds as a prison.

Freedom Summer was filled with violence. Some civil rights workers were shot at and **harassed**. Three workers, two white and one black, were murdered. Many more were arrested. But the summer also changed the attitudes and outlook of thousands of black Mississippians. For many blacks, especially those who lived in the countryside, it was the first time they had heard such a message of hope.

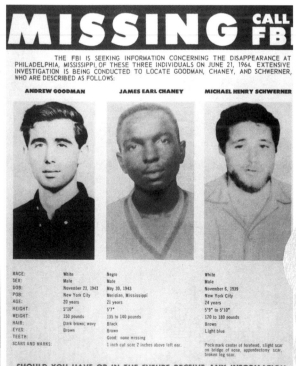

Three young civil rights workers, Andrew Goodman, James Earl Chaney and Michael Henry Schwerner, disappeared in Mississippi during June 1964. Their bodies were later found buried in a dam. A federal investigation discovered that members of the **Ku Klux Klan** were responsible for the murders.

Freedom Summer directly affected the attitudes of thousands of black Mississippians. Here Fannie Lou Hamer describes how a Freedom Summer volunteer changed her life.

Until then I'd never heard of no mass meeting and I didn't know that a Negro (African American) could register and vote. Bob Moses, Reffie Robinson, Jim Bevel, and James Forman were some of the SNCC workers who ran that meeting. When they asked for those to raise their hands who'd go down to the courthouse the next day, I raised mine. Had it up as high as I could get it. I guess if I'd had any sense I'd a-been a little scared, but what was the point of being scared? The only thing they could do to me was kill me and it seemed like they'd been trying to do that a little bit at a time ever since I could remember.

William Simmon's account
Many white Mississippians were infuriated by the volunteers. William Simmons, a spokesman for a White Citizens' Council, an organization that openly worked to preserve segregation, recalled how the volunteers angered a lot of people.

They were met with a feeling of some curiosity, but mostly resentment. They fanned out across the state, made a great to-do of breaking up our customs, of flouting social practices that had been respected by people here over the years. The arrogance they showed in wanting to reform the whole state created resentment. So to say they were not warmly received and welcomed is perhaps an understatement.

Civil Rights Act

As Freedom Summer was launched in Mississippi, members of **Congress** in Washington D.C. debated a new civil rights bill. President Kennedy, who was **assassinated** in November 1963, had failed to get any important civil rights laws passed. The new president, Lyndon B. Johnson from Texas, pledged his support for the new bill. The bill faced opposition in Congress, where many white lawmakers from the South were determined to vote against it. But after long and bitter debates, the bill was passed. Johnson signed it into law on 2 July 1964. The act was the most important set of laws passed for civil rights since **Reconstruction.** At last the South's **Jim Crow** laws would be dismantled.

The act made **discrimination** and **segregation** illegal and gave the **federal** government special powers to combat racial discrimination in education and employment. To many white supporters of the Civil Rights Movement, the Civil Rights Act was the final victory after a long period of protest and unrest. But for black Americans, the Civil Rights Act of 1964 was just the beginning.

President Lyndon B. Johnson, surrounded by dozens of supporters and journalists, signs the Civil Rights Act into law in 1964.

President Lyndon B. Johnson's speech

President Kennedy had submitted the Civil Rights Bill to Congress, but his assassination prevented him from turning the bill into law. It was his successor, President Lyndon B. Johnson, a southerner, who on 2 July 1964, signed the Civil Rights Act into law. Here is an excerpt from the speech that he gave on this momentous occasion.

Americans of every race and colour have died in battle to protect our freedom. Americans of every race and colour have worked to build a nation of widening opportunities. Now our generation of Americans has been called on to continue the unending search for justice within our own borders.

We believe that all men are created equal. Yet many are denied equal treatment.

We believe that all men have certain unalienable rights. Yet many Americans do not enjoy those rights.

We believe that all men are entitled to the blessings of liberty. Yet millions are being deprived of those blessings — not because of their own failures, but because of the colour of their skin.

The reasons are deeply imbedded in history and tradition and the nature of man. We can understand — without rancor or hatred — how this all happened.

But it cannot continue. Our Constitution, the foundation of our Republic, forbids it. The principles of our freedom forbid it. Morality forbids it. And the law I will sign tonight forbids it.

Slow to change

The Civil Rights Act was a great victory, but it caused a huge backlash. Many white Americans were still not ready to treat black people as equals. In the South, the **Ku Klux Klan** continued to use violence to attack blacks who challenged **segregation**. Other groups, called White Citizens' Councils, worked to preserve segregation, defending it as 'our way of life'. White candidates for office said that they would never let the walls of segregation fall. Many of them were voted in with overwhelming support.

Civil rights **activists** tried to register blacks to vote. Blacks who did faced **harassment**. When they showed up to vote, they were quizzed about American history or asked to explain portions of the **Constitution**. If they failed to answer correctly they were denied the right to vote. Others were ordered to pay a tax, which few could afford. Whites rarely faced such hurdles.

The first demonstrators who tried to march from Selma to Montgomery were stopped by state police. In a few terrifying moments, state police attacked the demonstrators with tear gas and clubs. This woman collapsed after being overwhelmed by tear gas.

As a result few blacks could vote. In Selma, Alabama, for example, only 156 of the city's 15,000 eligible black residents were registered. In March 1965, King led protests in Selma. After violent clashes with the police, King announced he would lead an 86-kilometre (54-mile) march through Alabama to the state capital of Montgomery. The march put pressure on law makers to act. In 1965, **Congress** passed the Voting Rights Act, which removed most of the barriers that prevented blacks from registering and voting.

Protest songs

An observer of a civil rights protest could usually count on hearing at least one common thing – a song. Many protest songs came from black churches. One song, called 'We Shall Overcome', has been called the **anthem** of the Civil Rights Movement. The words came from a gospel song written by Charles Tindley in 1900.

We shall overcome
We shall overcome
We shall overcome some day
Oh deep in my heart
I do believe
We shall overcome some day.

Malcolm X and black power

By the mid-1960s, the mood in the United States had soured. Many whites were losing patience with the Civil Rights Movement, declaring that it had already achieved its aims. Blacks, in the meantime, were angered by the lack of progress. Despite new laws, blacks still suffered from a lack of good jobs, as well as poor schools and housing.

It was worse in the cities, where large black populations lived in crowded neighbourhoods well away from jobs and services. In their view the Civil Rights Movement was failing. In 1965, their anger exploded into riots. The Watts region of Los Angeles was devastated in four days of burning and looting. Thirty-four people were killed and thousands injured. In the following years, race riots ravaged dozens of US cities.

Some black leaders, such as Malcolm X and Stokely Carmichael, wanted a new 'black power' movement. Their ideas were more violent and aggressive than King's and the student peace-centred movements. They also urged black Americans to take pride in themselves and in the achievements of black American culture.

Black American rage at the slow pace of change and poverty in inner cities exploded into riots during the late 1960s. In this photograph, police search black American youths during riots in the Watts region of Los Angeles.

Malcolm X delivers a speech in Harlem in May 1963. Eloquent and passionate, Malcolm X urged black Americans to take greater pride in themselves and their community and to battle against white injustice.

The words of Malcolm X

Malcolm X in his writings and speeches often criticized the non-violent approach of other campaigners like Martin Luther King. He argued that the use of violence, as a means of self-defence, was justifiable. After 1964 he began to moderate some of his views. In 1965 he was **assassinated**.

The common goal of 22 million Afro-Americans is respect as human beings, the God-given right to be a human being. Our common goal is to obtain the human rights that America has been denying us. We can never get civil rights in America until our human rights are first restored. We will never be recognized as citizens there until we are first recognized as humans.

I believe in the brotherhood of man, all men, but I don't believe in brotherhood with anybody who doesn't want brotherhood with me. I believe in treating people right, but I'm not going to waste my time trying to treat somebody right who doesn't know how to return the treatment.

Assassinations and riots

In the late 1960s, the United States experienced more unrest as thousands of US soldiers were fighting and dying in the Asian country of South Vietnam. Its supporters said it was a necessary war to prevent the spread of **communism**. But many Americans openly disagreed and tens of thousands of them protested in the streets.

As the debate over the war raged, King and other civil rights leaders continued to demonstrate for equal rights. In 1966, King went to Chicago to protest about **segregated** housing and the lack of services for the city's black residents. When he led demonstrations into areas where whites lived, King was stunned by the angry taunting and resistance of the white crowds.

Through 1967 and 1968, riots and unrest shook US cities. On 4 April 1968, King was **assassinated** on his hotel balcony in Memphis, Tennessee. The killing shocked the United States and condolences poured in from around the world.

By the end of the 1960s, the Civil Rights Movement had broken into several groups with different goals and different ideas. One was a group called the 'Black Panthers', who urged black Americans to withdraw from white society and use violence, if necessary, to protect themselves.

The assassination of Martin Luther King robbed the nation of one of its most eloquent and respected defenders of civil rights. Here, at his funeral in Atlanta, thousands follow the simple wagon that carried his coffin to the cemetery.

Elaine Brown describes members of the Black Panther Party

The Black Panther Party was founded in Oakland, California, in 1966 to protect black residents from police brutality. Elaine Brown, who in 1974 became the first woman to lead the Black Panther Party, describes the party's membership.

The party reached out mostly to men, to young, black urban men who were on the streets, who knew that there were no options somewhere in their lives, who were gang members because that was all you could be in order to find some sense of dignity about yourself. We reached out to these people because we had something for them to do with the rest of their lives. In most cases, they were used to violence, they were used to struggle, they were used to fighting just to keep alive. We offered them the opportunity to make their lives meaningful.

This Black Panther poster from the 1960s shows the gesture of 'Black Power' – a raised left fist. The Black Panther movement urged black Americans to look back to their origins in Africa for pride and strength.

Civil rights in the 1970s, 1980s and 1990s

In the decades after the peak of the Civil Rights Movement, black leaders continued to fight for **equality**. In some cases, black Americans were in worse situations in the 1970s than before the movement arose in the 1950s. A strong black middle class of professionals developed, then moved away from their black communities. The communities that remained often became isolated within cities and began disintegrating under the pressures of crime, drugs and lack of employment. **Discrimination** remained a reality for most blacks.

But blacks also experienced astonishing success, such as would have been unimaginable in the 1950s and 1960s. Scarcely more than 100 black Americans held elected positions when the Voting Rights Act was passed in 1965. In 1989, 7200 elected positions were held by blacks. Almost 5000 of these positions were in the South.

Programmes such as **affirmative action** opened up schools of higher education to more and more black students. Black Americans began to occupy very visible positions of power and authority. In the 1970s Barbara Jordan became a highly respected member of **Congress**. Colin Powell, a black army general, became Chairman of the Joint Chiefs of Staff – the highest position in the US Army – and oversaw the Gulf War of 1991. He later became Secretary of State for the USA. In 2000 Condoleezza Rice was appointed US National Security Advisor by President George W. Bush.

Decades after the Civil Rights Movement, black Americans have begun to occupy positions of power in the United States that would have been blocked to them during the 1950s and 1960s. Here, Colin Powell addresses members of the press after being sworn in as US Secretary of State.

Luke Harris's experience

Luke Harris, an **attorney**, describes the benefits of affirmative action in education, which enabled him to go to university. He received a law degree from Yale University in 1977.

For me, the whole era of affirmative action was something that I saw as representing hope, as representing encouragement, and as representing a chance that American society was going, at least in some kind of way, for the first time in its history to allow people of color to be in a position where their individual capabilities ... could flower and blossom in ways that had never been the case over the centuries. Without affirmative action, there is no doubt that I would not have been able to go to Saint Joe's. I worked very hard and I wound up graduating number one in my department, and that's when I wound up with the opportunity to go to Yale Law School. So I went to Yale Law School, feeling that I was part of the crest of a social movement. And that American society was finally opening up in some limited ways to allow people of color and blacks in particular to participate in all aspects of American life. It had never happened before in America. And I felt proud and I still do feel proud to be a part of that process.

The unfinished revolution

In the decades since the Civil Rights Movement, people's opinions about race and **equality** have certainly changed. As the USA is largely a nation of **immigrants** it is important that the civil rights of all those immigrants and the rights of the original inhabitants, the Native American peoples, are recognized. Americans used to insist that newcomers join the American 'melting pot' – that is merge their identity and **assimilate** with the white majority. Today, the melting pot has become more of a 'mosaic'. Although people of different racial origin still tend naturally to live together, people are moving, mixing and settling into new communities more than they have ever done before. The flood of Latino (people from the former Spanish colonies of South and Central America), Caribbean blacks and Asian immigrants coming into the United States over the past 40 years has changed the country from black-white to a nation of many colours.

Black Americans still suffer from poverty and **discrimination**, more than other Americans, but many thousands graduate from college and move into high-level positions as doctors, lawyers and managers of powerful companies.

Impossible in the years before the Civil Rights Movement, this African American teacher can now enjoying reading a story to a group of children from different racial backgrounds.

Declaration from the Black Radical Congress
A group of black American political **activists**,
called the Black Radical Congress, met in March
1997 to discuss how to advance civil rights. Below
is an excerpt from their declaration, stating that
much remains to be done.

Resistance is in our marrow as Black people,
given our history in this place. From the
Haitian revolution, to the US abolitionist
movement against slavery, to the twentieth
century movement for civil rights and
empowerment we have struggled and died
for justice.

We believe that the struggle must continue,
and with renewed vigor. Our historical
experiences suggest to us ... what a truly just
and democratic society should look like: It
should be democratic, not just in myth but
in practice, a society in which all people —
regardless of color ethnicity [race], religion,
nationality, national origin, sex, sexual
orientation, age, family structure, or mental
or physical capability — enjoy full human
rights, the fruits of their labor, and the
freedom to realize their full human potential.

What have we learnt from the Civil Rights Movement?

At different times in history, people have risen to challenge their rulers about the way they are forced to live. It is often a tragic story with a tragic ending. As people on both sides grow angry, they pick up spears, swords or guns to get their way. The conflict becomes bitter and violent. People are wounded and die, homes and cities are destroyed.

The Civil Rights Movement, like other movements of its kind, could have ended this way. The Movement faced furious opposition. Anyone who took part in the Movement, from a single demonstrator to the highest leader, faced possible death. But the Civil Rights Movement as a whole did not turn violent. Instead, the Movement demanded only what was just – that the United States live up to its own ideals as stated in the Declaration of Independence that 'all men are created equal'.

By using **non-violent** tactics, the Movement confronted **racism** in a way that stirred the conscience of society and changed the hearts as well as the minds of many people. Today – in government, in schools, in places where Americans work and live – the impact of the Civil Rights Movement is visible. It demonstrates that people who look different and who hold different beliefs can still come together to be part of the same community.

On the 37th anniversary of King's 'I Have a Dream' speech, the black American community could be pleased with the progress in American race relations, while also acknowledging the work remaining to be done. Here, protesters bring attention to the problem of police brutality and 'racial profiling', during which black Americans are stopped by police because of their race.

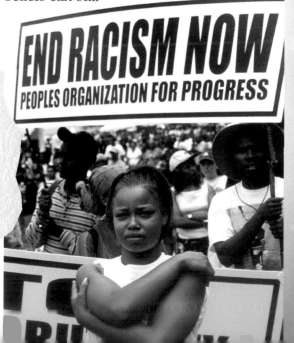

Barbara Jordan's speech

Barbara Jordan rose from an impoverished childhood in Texas to become a member of the **House of Representatives**. In 1976, she became the first black American woman to deliver the keynote (most important) address at a political convention. In 1994 she was awarded the Presidential Medal of Freedom, the nation's highest civilian honour. Below is part of Jordan's keynote address to the Democratic Party Convention, held in New York City in July 1976.

In the past it would have been most unusual for any national political party to ask that a Barbara Jordan deliver a keynote address ... but tonight here I am. And I feel that . . . my presence here is one additional bit of evidence that the American Dream need not forever be deferred.

We are a people in search of our future. We are a people in search of a national community.

We are attempting to fulfill our national purpose; to create and sustain a society in which all of us are equal.

In this election year we must define the common good and begin again to shape a common good and . . . a common future ... A spirit of harmony will survive in America only if each of us remembers that we share a common destiny.

Now, I began this speech by commenting to you on the uniqueness of a Barbara Jordan making the keynote address. Well I am going to close my speech by quoting a Republican President and I ask you that as you listen to these words of Abraham Lincoln, you relate them to the concept of national community in which every last one of us participates:

'As I would not be a slave, so I would not be a master. This expresses my idea of Democracy. Whatever differs from this, to the extent of the difference is no Democracy.'

Timeline

1619   First African slaves are unloaded from a Dutch ship at the English colony of Virginia in North America.

1800s   Slavery becomes the basis of social and economic life in the United States. Slaves, freed blacks, and **abolitionists** use various methods to protest against slavery. Slavery is virtually abolished in the northern states by 1860.

1861–1865 American Civil War.

1863   January: President Abraham Lincoln signs the Emancipation Proclamation as the nation fights a bloody **civil war**. The document legally frees slaves throughout the **rebelling** southern states.

1864–1877 **Reconstruction** in the southern states. Black Americans receive many rights, but gradually lose them as southern whites retake power.

1896   **Supreme Court** ruling upholds segregation in *Plessy vs Ferguson* case.

1909   The National Association for the Advancement of Colored People is founded by blacks and whites, to fight **discrimination** against black Americans.

1954   May: The Supreme Court issues its landmark decision, *Brown vs. Board of Education, Topeka, Kansas*. The decision rules that **segregated** education is unequal.

1955   December: Rosa Parks is arrested in Montgomery, Alabama, for refusing to give up her bus seat to a white man. Black Americans begin **boycotting** public buses in Montgomery to protest segregation. The boycott lasts more than a year and ends on 20 December 1956, when the Supreme Court upholds a decision that segregation on the buses is illegal.

1956   September: Nine black students are turned away by state troops at Little Rock High School in Little Rock, Arkansas. President Dwight Eisenhower orders **federal** soldiers to the high school to guard the students as they attend school.

1960   The first sit-in is held in Greensboro, North Carolina. The tactic is soon imitated by several other groups and is used throughout the United States to fight segregation.

1961   May: The first 'Freedom Riders' ride buses through the South to protest segregation on interstate bus travel. The riders face a combination of mob violence and **harassment** by local police.

1963   Spring: Martin Luther King Jr. leads protests in Birmingham, Alabama, against segregation. After he is arrested, King pens the 'Letter from a Birmingham Jail'. August: Martin Luther King gives his 'I Have A Dream' speech at the foot of the Lincoln Memorial in Washington D.C.

1964   July: President Lyndon B. Johnson signs the wide-ranging Civil Rights Act. 'Freedom Summer' takes place in Mississippi when civil rights **activists** invite thousands of students to enter the state and register black residents to vote.

1965   March: Martin Luther King and other civil rights leaders organize protests in Selma, Alabama against voting restrictions. The protests meet bitter resistance. August: The Watts region of Los Angeles is torn by riots. Riots continue to shake US cities through the rest of the 1960s. Voting Rights Act is signed into law. The act makes it illegal to deny the right to vote because of the voter's wealth or race.

1966	The Black Panther Party is founded in Oakland, California.
1968	April: Martin Luther King is **assassinated** in Memphis, Tennessee.
1970s and 1980s	Fairer admission and **affirmative action** programmes increase the number of blacks at the nation's centres of higher education.
1986	January: Martin Luther King's birthday is honoured for the first time as a federal holiday. It is observed every year on the third Monday in January.

Find out more

Books & websites

Causes and Consequences of The African-American Civil Rights Movement, Michael Webber, (Evans, 1997)

Days That Shook the World: the Dream of Martin Luther King, Liz Gogerly, (Hodder Wayland, 2003)

Leading Lives: Martin Luther King Jr., David Downing, (Heinemann Library, 2002)

Living in Crisis: Civil Rights Movement, Nigel Richie, (Hodder Wayland, 2002)

Martin Luther King (Judge for Yourself), Christine Hatt, (Evans, 2002)

Go Exploring! Log on to Heinemann's online history resource.
www.heinemannexplore.co.uk

http://www.lib.virginia.edu/speccol/exhibits/music/protest_overcome.html
Lift Every Voice: Protest Songs

http://www.nps.gov/malu/
Martin Luther King National Historic Site

http://www.nps.gov/brvb/
Brown V. Board of Education National Historic Site

http://www.cr.nps.gov/nr/travel/civilrights/index.htm
We Shall Overcome: Historic Places of the Civil Rights Movement

List of primary sources

The author and publisher gratefully acknowledge the following publications and websites from which written sources in the book are drawn. In some cases the wording or sentence structure has been simplified to make the material more appropriate for a school readership.

P.9 Olaudah Equiano: *The Interesting Narrative and Other Writings*: Ed Vincent Carretta (Penguin, 1995)

P.11 Henry Bibb: *Slave Testimony*: John W. Blassingame (Baton Rouge: Louisiana State Press, 1977)

P.13 Robert Purvis: *Slave Testimony*: John W. Blassingame (Baton Rouge: Louisiana State Press, 1977)

P.15 We Shall Overcome: Historic Places of the Civil Rights Movement: http//www.cr.nps.gov/nr/travel/civilrights/change.htm

P.17 Ralph Abernathy: *Voices of Freedom*: Henry Hampton and Steve Fayer (Bantam Books, 1990)

P.19 Earl Warren: *Eyes on the Prize*: Juan Williams (Penguin Books, 1987)

P.21 Rosa Parks: *My Soul Is Rested: Movement Days in the Deep South Remembered*: Howell Raines (G.P. Putnam's and Sons, 1977)

P.23 Jo Ann Robinson and Virginia Durr: *Eyes on the Prize*: Juan Williams (Penguin Books, 1987)

P.25 Elizabeth Eckford: *The Long Shadow of Little Rock*: Daisy Gates (University of Arkansas Pr; ISBN: 0938626752 Reprint edition, 1987)

P.27 Franklin McCain: *My Soul Is Rested: Movement Days in the Deep South Remembered*: Howell Raines (G.P. Putnam's and Sons, 1977)

P.29 Jim Zwerg: *Eyes on the Prize*: Juan Williams (Penguin Books, 1987)

P.31 Martin Luther King Jr.: I Have A Dream. Writings and speeches that changed the world: Ed James M. Washington (Harper Collins, 1992)

P.33 PBS (Public Broadcasting Service) online site for the program: *The American Experience: the Presidents*: http://www.pbs.org/wgbh/amex/presidents/nf/resource/ken/primdocs/civilrights.html

P.35 Martin Luther King Jr.: I Have A Dream. Writings and speeches that changed the world: Ed James M. Washington (Harper Collins, 1992)

P.37 Fannie Lou Hamer: taped interview by Julius Lester and Maria Varela of the SNCC (1967). William Simmons: *Eyes on the Prize*: Juan Williams (Penguin Books, 1987)

P.39 President Lyndon B. Johnson: Lyndon Baines Johnson Library and Museum: National Archives and Records Administration: The Link: http://www.lbjlib.utexas.edu/Johnson/archives.hom/speeches.hom/640702.asp

P.41 Charles Tyndley: 'We Shall Overcome', 1900

P.43 Malcolm X: http//www.cmgww.com/historic/malcolm/

P.45 Elaine Brown: *Voices of Freedom*: Hampton, Henry and Steve Fayer, (Bantam Books, 1990)

P.47 Luke Harris: *Voices of Freedom*: Hampton, Henry and Steve Fayer, (Bantam Books, 1990)

P.49 Black Radical Congress: *Let Nobody Turn Us Around*: Ed Manning Marable and Leith Mullings (Rowman & Littlefield Publishers, Inc., 2000)

P.51 Barbara Jordan: Democratic Convention Keynote Address: http://www.elf.net/bjordan/keynote.html

Glossary

abolition forcible ending (a law or custom)

activist person who works for a certain cause or issue

affirmative action program implemented in the 1960s in the United States that gives preferences in jobs and education to various groups, including women and black Americans, because they suffered from racism and discrimination

anthem song that becomes a symbol of a movement, government, or organization

artefact object, made and used by people, that comes from a certain historical period

assassinate murder a person, especially for political reasons

assimilate incorporate the social customs beliefs, etc., of another cultural group

attorney US lawyer who acts on behalf of others in legal matters

bondage condition of being kept at work or in a place unwillingly

boycott protest organized by people who try to cause change by deliberately not buying or using something

civil disobedience deliberate breaking of a law because it is unfair. The purpose is to bring attention to the law and help overturn it.

civil war war between groups of people from the same country

communism political system in which private ownership is abolished and industries and services are run by the state

Congress US government body that makes new laws. It consists of the House of Representatives and the Senate.

constitution set of guiding principles written down, which state how a country is to be governed

desegregation removing the laws that separate people of one race from another

discrimination treating some people worse than others, because of their race or gender, for example

empower to give authority or power to

equality situation in which people all have the same rights and opportunities

federal relating to the national government in the USA, or of any other union of states

harass annoy repeatedly, torment

House of Representatives one of the two elected bodies that make up the US system of government

immigrant person who leaves one country to settle in another

Jim Crow term used to describe the racially segregated society created by law in the late nineteenth century in the South. The term came from a fictional character who was an old, black slave.

Ku Klux Klan group formed after the American Civil War that was determined to keep whites in power and keep black Americans and white Americans separate, using terrorist tactics

legislation group of laws passed for approval to the governing body of a country

migrant worker worker who moves from place to place to do seasonal work

non-violence refusal to use force when dealing with others, even if they are violent

picketing protesting outside the premises of an organization considered responsible for an injustice

plantation large crop-farming estate that can employ hundreds of people

primary sources documents, photographs, or objects that are directly connected to a historical event or period

racism discrimination against people solely on the basis of their race

rally public meeting to discuss and bring attention to an issue

rebellion defiance of the existing order or way of doing things, usually with violence

Reconstruction period after the American Civil War when the former Confederate states were brought back into the Union

secede withdraw from a union or existing order

secondary source second-hand account of an event

segregation separation of two or more races in public spaces through law and custom

Supreme Court the highest, most powerful and final decision-maker of federal laws in the United States

unbiased not allowing personal opinion to affect judgement

Union the grouping together of the United States

Index

Abernathy, Reverend Ralph 17
'affirmative action' in education 46–7
American Civil War 12–13

Bethune, Mary McLeod 16
Birmingham, Alabama
   civil rights protests 32
   segregation 30–1
Black Panther Party 44–5
Black power 42–3
Black Radical Congress 49

Carmichael, Stokely 42
Civil Rights Act (1964) 38–9
Congress of Racial Equality (CORE) 28

Douglass, Frederick 10
Du Bois, W.E.B 16

Eckford, Elizabeth 24–5
Eisenhower, President Dwight 24–5
Equiano, Olaudah 9

Freedom Rides 28–9
Freedom Summer 36–7

Gandhi, Mohandas 26

Harlan, Supreme Court Justice John
   Marshall 15

Jim Crow laws 14–15, 38
Johnson, President Lyndon B 38–9
Jordan, Barbara 46, 51

Kennedy, President John F. 6, 7, 32–3
   assassination 38
Ku Klux Klan 14, 36, 40

Lincoln, Abraham 12, 51
Little Rock High School, Arkansas 25–6
Los Angeles, riots in 42
Luther King Jr., Martin 4, 5, 20, 22–3,
   30–1, 34–5, 40, 43, 50
   assassination 5, 44

Malcolm X 42–3
March on Washington 34–5
Montgomery bus boycott 22–3
Montgomery Improvement Association
   (MIA) 22

National Association for the
   Advancement of Colored People
   (NAACP) 16, 18

Parks, Rosa 20–21
Powell, Colin 46

Reconstruction 12
Rice, Condoleezza 46

segregation 14–17, 26–31
   in schools 18–19
   on buses 20–21
Selma to Montgomery march 5, 40
sit-ins 26–7
slavery 8–13
Southern Christian Leadership
   Conference (SCLC) 22, 30
Student Non-violent Coordinating
   Committee (SNCC) 26

Turner, Nat 10

Vietnam War 44
Voting rights 5, 36–7, 40
Voting Rights Act (1965) 40, 46

Warren, Supreme Court Justice Earl 18
Washington, Booker T 16
White Citizens' Council 37, 40
World War I 16